ARCHITECTURAL JOURNEYS

WITHDRAWN

ARCHITECTURAL JOURNEYS

Antoine Predock

Compiled by Brad Collins and Elizabeth Zimmermann

RIZZOLI
NEW YORK

First published in the United States of America in 1995 by
Rizzoli International Publications, Inc.
300 Park Avenue South, New York, New York 10010

Predock, Antoine.
   Architectural journeys / Antoine Predock ; compiled by Bradford P. Collins.
      p. cm.
   ISBN 0-8478-1904-3
   1. Predock, Antoine—Themes, motives. I. Collins, Brad. II. Title.
NA737.P67A4 1995
720'.92—dc20   95-16919
                                                     CIP

Cover Image: Agadir Palm Bay Resort and Casino, Agadir, Morocco

Endpapers: American Heritage Center and Art Museum, University of Wyoming at Laramie

All photographic documentation by Mary Elkins and Robert Reck.

Design and Composition:
   Group C Inc/ New Haven
     BC, CK, JR, FS, EZ

Printed and bound in Italy

To Constance

Drawing, for me, is both a vehicle for understanding and a gestural act unto itself. Recording an experience via drawing embodies much more than an analytical intention. In fact, my drawings aren't very analytical. When I draw historic buildings, they are inaccurate in many ways. My drawings are close, but they aren't about detail or proportion. They are about the spirit of a building or a place, and the spirit embedded in the encounter and its translation. Drawing is a way of taking on a place, absorbing it, immersing myself in it.

I see the making of architecture and traveling as one interwoven experience. Assimilating different places, observing the atmospheres in different locales in the world, both real and imagined, are all journeys. These assimilations and observations accumulate and comprise the foreground for making architecture. The journeys began while I was a student and continue now.

While making my early drawings, during the 1960s in particular, I was traveling on my motorcycle with only the bare essentials. I carried only a sketchbook and India ink, and used objects I found on the site as drawing tools—bird feathers or twigs or Popsicle sticks I sharpened with a knife. Whatever was there, I drew with. An important part of the encounter was actually finding these artifacts and drawing with them. Later, I added a tiny watercolor kit; all I had to do was carry a small bottle of water and that little kit. I didn't start making brush drawings with pastel until I discovered the brush pen, which

is easy to travel with because it involves no clean-up.

When I was traveling in Europe, I would draw some buildings over and over again. I drew Chartres ten different times. Sometimes when I draw a building, especially one I've done over and over again from one vantage point, like the Pantheon, it becomes burned into my system as if it were a signature. I sign the building. I haven't analyzed the building, but I have felt it and I have translated it. I often think that my drawing, the physical act of drawing, in terms of comfort level and freedom, should correspond closely to how I sign my name. Yet there is something mysterious about a great building that is beyond a mere graphic encounter. When I spend so much time with a building, the accumulation of discoveries is very powerful.

Sometimes the traveling relates very directly to a project I am doing, in the sense of encountering a new place and translating it in different ways. The translation can occur through various media, ranging from collage—assembling postcards, magazines, currency, etc.—to drawing, to literature. The graphic translation is primarily collaged images combined with drawings, sometimes twenty feet long by three or four feet wide, usually on butcher paper or wrapping paper. The drawings range from very obvious travel sketches to cryptic anticipatory drawings of what a building may be, a kind of encoding or DNA that will inform the making of the building. Literature has a great influence on my initial encounter, especially the poetic recounting of experiences particular to different places—the writings of Willa Cather on New Mexico, Camus on North Africa, Bruce Chatwin on Australia or Patagonia, and Federico García Lorca's evocations of Andalucia.

My translations are sometimes very elaborate and complex because I need to encode as much information as possible into what I am doing. Color, script, and annotated collage material that often involves foreign language serve as references to remind me of particular physical and cultural icons. This kind of mixed-media immersion is something I have always liked to do and always have done. The drawings are essential to introducing a project to my team and having them live it with me; they constitute a critical starting point in the collective process.

Reading a site, with the prospect of building on it, is an all-at-once experience that involves understanding factors such as wind, sun, environmental impact, and cultural strata, but that simultaneously entails imagining the lives the site might lead—a kind of time-travel encounter. Sometimes a very reductive mark will follow. As I define, think about, and live in the site, anything can fill up the crevices in the interstitial realm I am creating. My connection to the site strengthens as I begin to translate it.

When I finally make a mark—a drawing, a collage, a clay model—it's a very informed circumstance that is different from the innocence of an encounter with a great building or a landscape while traveling, or looking out the window of an airplane. The physical act of making the mark feels the same, but the stage is set differently.

When the project is formative or embryonic, the drawings are often terse and immediate. They can be the first impulses toward what I consider my most significant drawing medium (though it's hard to call it a drawing), the clay model. Preliminary or anticipatory drawings lead to these three-dimensional clay models, which can be very tiny, three-by-five inches, like Cal Poly, or very large, like the one for Agadir, which is five feet long and three feet wide. I am still exploring as I work with the clay, but I am working toward a finality. Compared to a drawing on paper the models are very real; they are the building. They are not "massing models," they rationally address section and plan. I work from two- or three-dimensional program cut-outs, just abstract blocks or pieces

of paper that indicate areas for program elements and square footage that must be accommodated in the building, and I refer to those continually while I'm working the clay. The gestural imperative with a clay model is so close to drawing that I can't separate the two. Physically making a drawing mark feels the same as making a cut in the clay. I don't make the models by molding the clay, I cut the clay with a special knife that makes clean, sharp cuts. In clay there are no limits—no orthogonal constraints, no angular limitations, no limitations on curvilinear moves. It is as liquid as a drawing.

UC Davis is one of my most successful clay models. My initial cut in the clay was the curve that runs through the site, and that cut is exactly replicated in the actual building. It is the most explicit diagram of my intention about the three-dimensional encounter with a site—excavating into the earth with pieces of the building angling toward the sky. Almost all of the most recent, completed work—Cal Poly at Pomona, American Heritage Center, Los Alamos, Thousand Oaks, Ventana Vista—started with

a clay model. The models are encoded directly and immediately into computer files. I insist that this is done in the most accurate way. These models are very precise representations of the building.

The models and the two-dimensional drawings are a record of the journey through the project—the exploration of the imagined sites that parallel a physical site and accrue to it conceptually. A journey of the imagination thus becomes an architectural journey, too; but since I may invent these conceptual layers, the outcome is specific compared to the random foraging, collecting, and absorbing that occurs while traveling. There are two different outcomes, but both are journeys.

My journeys never seem to be those of a tourist; they always seem to be those of an architect. Anything I see or hear or feel or smell, everything that I encounter is lodged in my system and has an impact on the buildings I am going to make, although I may not know what these are at the time. Travel is a journey that becomes a prediction, something latent that appears later in the process of making a building.

12 Rio Grande Valley, New Mexico, *1961*

14 Madrigal de las Altas Torres, Spain, *1962*

Monasterio de Guisando, Spain, *1962* 15

Plaza Mayor, Salamanca, Spain, *1962*   17

18 Acropolis, Athens, *1962, 1983*

20   Leon Cathedral, Spain, *1962*

Zaragoza, Spain, *1962*   21

Seville Cathedral, Spain, *1963* Malaga Cathedral, Spain, *1963* 23

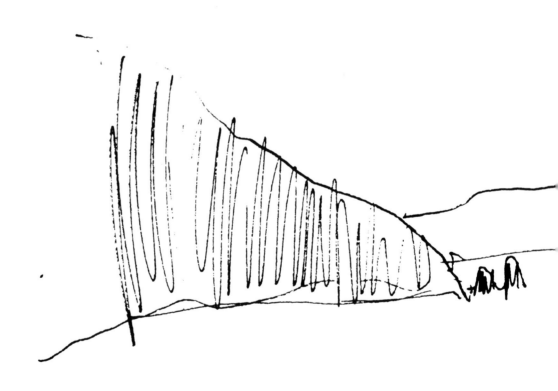

24 Costa Blanca, Spain, *1963*

26 Monte Albán, Mexico, *1964*

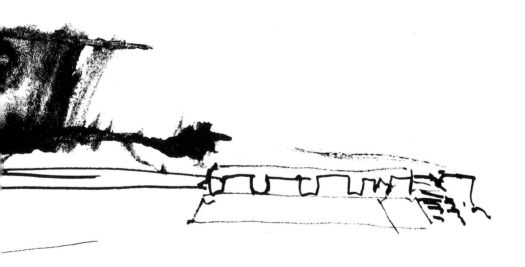

Teotihuacán, Mexico, *1964*   27

28　Chaco Canyon, New Mexico, *1964*

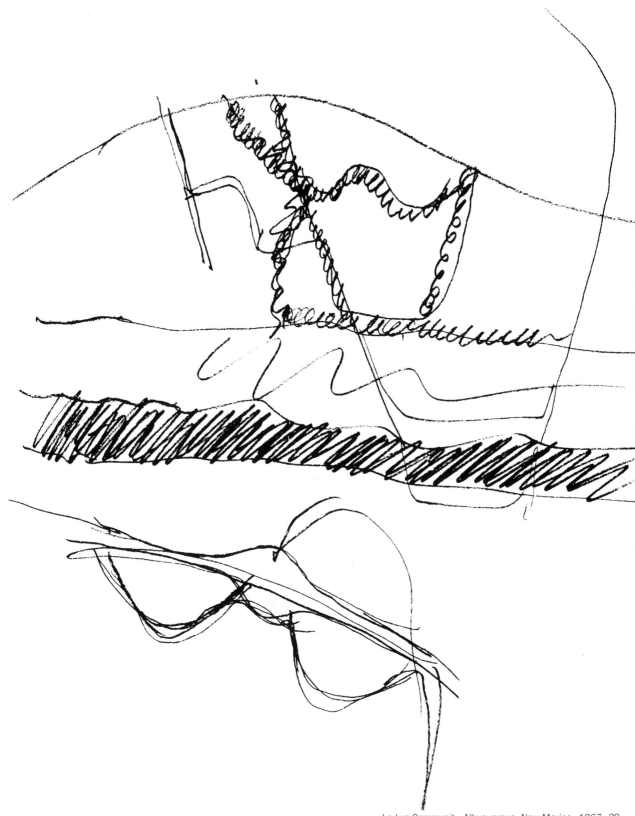

La Luz Community, Albuquerque, New Mexico, *1967* 29

34   Rocamadour, France, *1982*

36 Segovia, Spain, *1982*

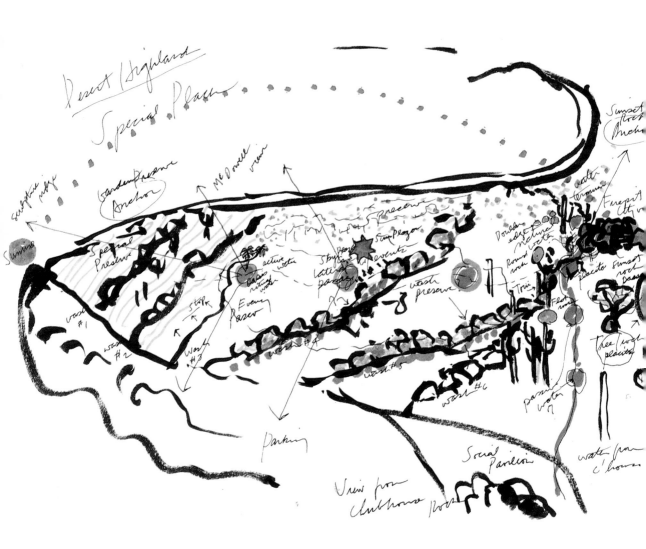

38   Desert Highlands, Phoenix, Arizona, *1983*

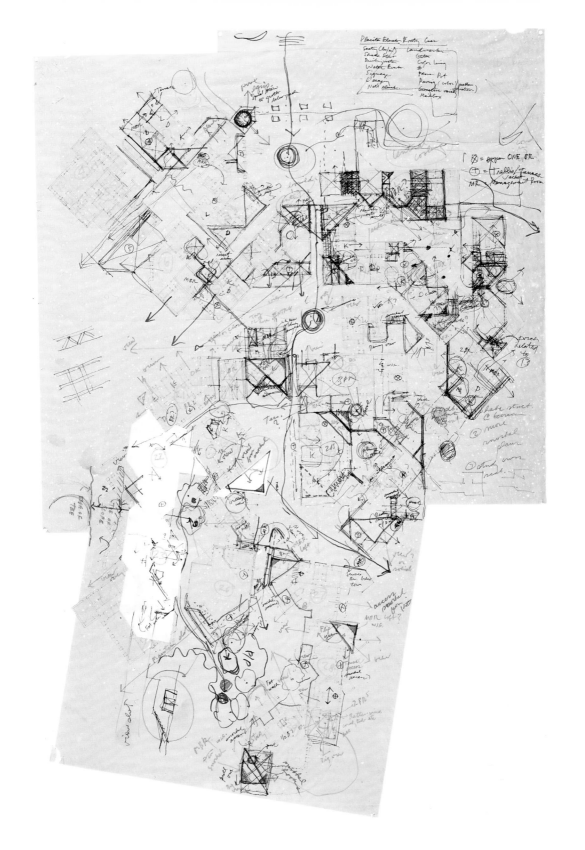

40   Les Baux de Provence, France, *1982*

42　Il Tempietto, Rome, *1985*

Trinità dei Monti, Rome, *1985*   43

Porta Maggiore, Rome, *1985*   47

48   Porta Maggiore, Rome, *1985*

Tomb of Eurysaces, Rome, *1985* 49

50 Tuscolo, Italy, *1985*

52   Mount Etna, Italy, *1985*

54   Grotto of Tiberius, Italy, *1985*

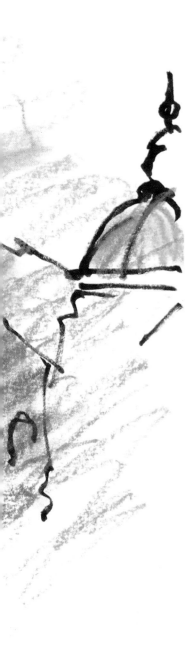

Temple of Apollo, Rome   Temple of Castor and Pollux, Rome, *1985*   59

60 Hadrian's Villa, Tivoli, Italy, *1985*

Pyramid of Caio Cestio, Rome, *1985* 63

64   Nelson Fine Arts Center, Arizona State University at Tempe, *1985*

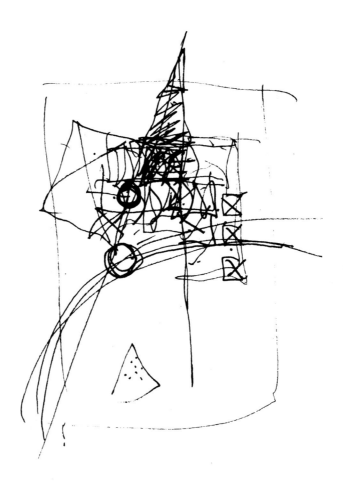

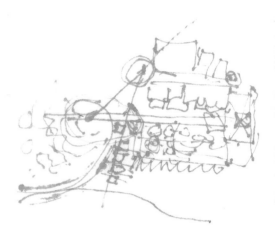

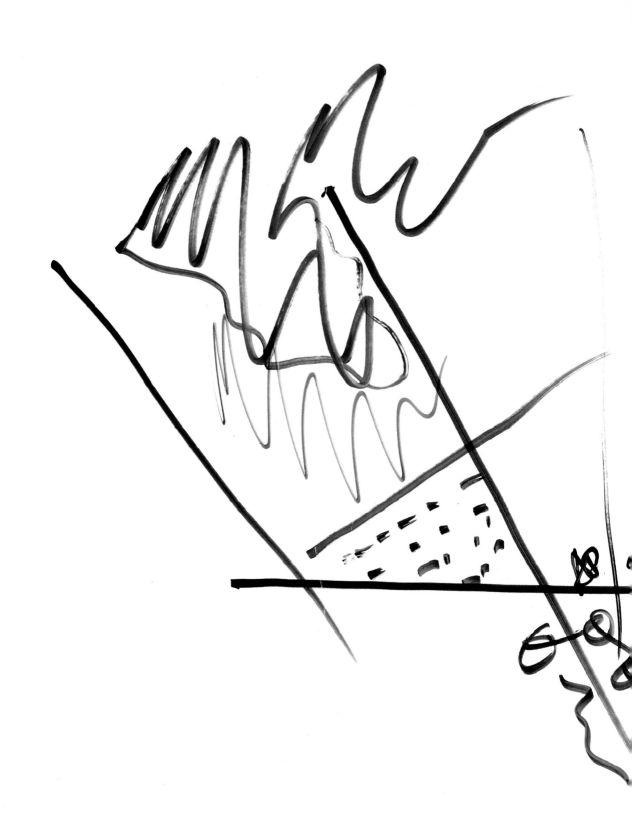

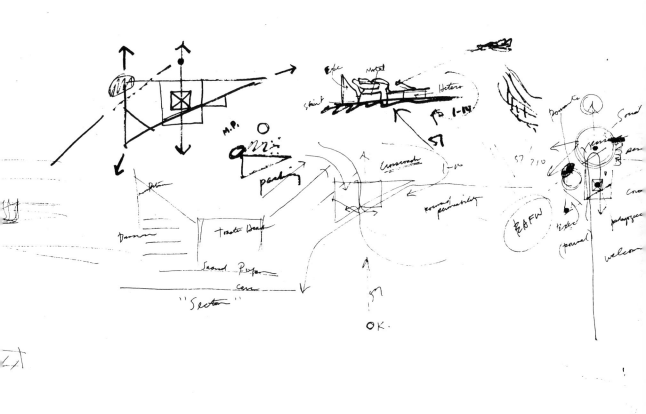

Classroom, Laboratory, Administration Building, *1987*   77

Trail of light
Dwell in Trees
Many Galleries
Dining Treehouse
A Blind
Birds above
Secret Garden

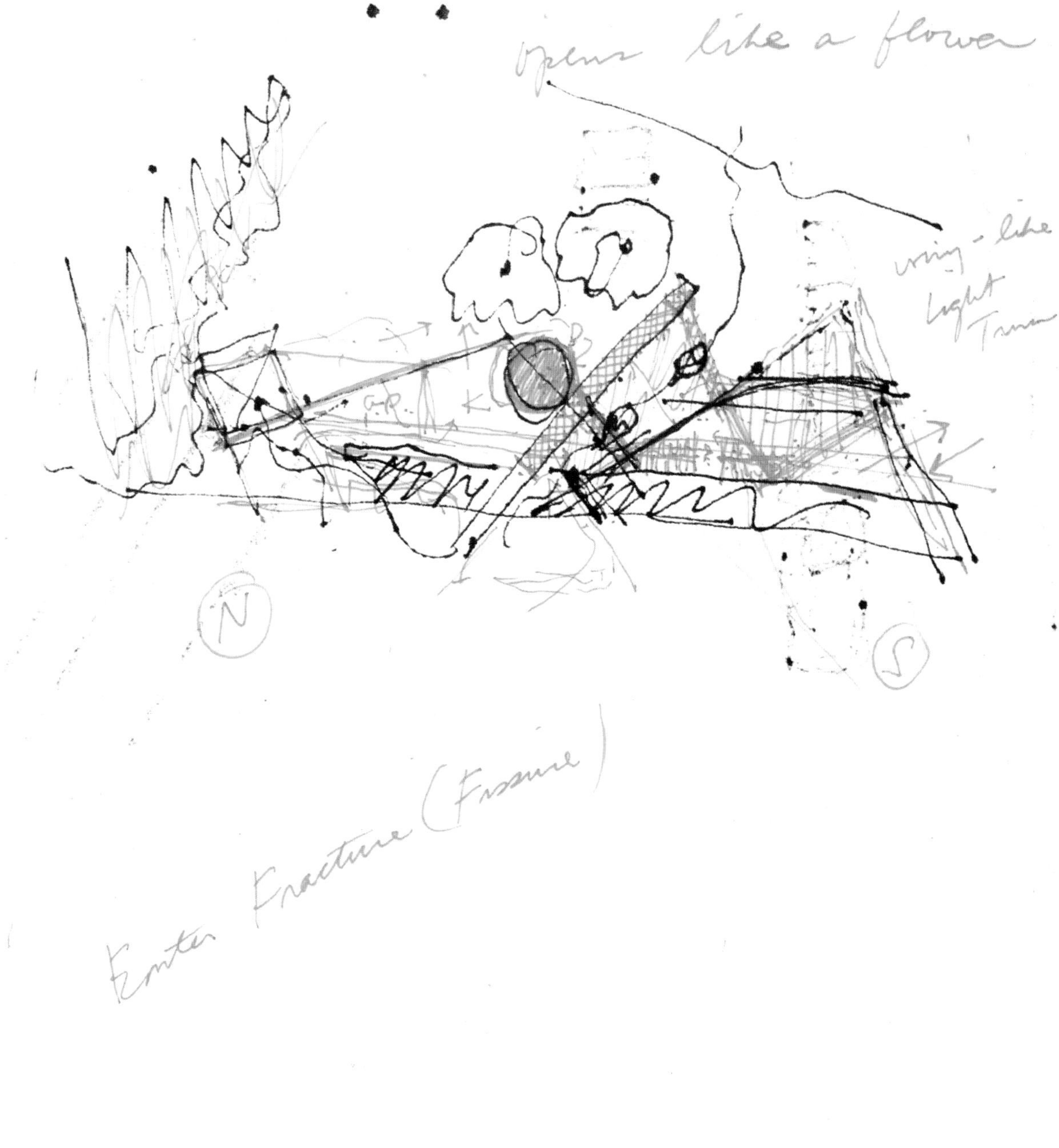

opens like a flower

wing-like light Truss

N

S

Enter Fracture (Fissure)

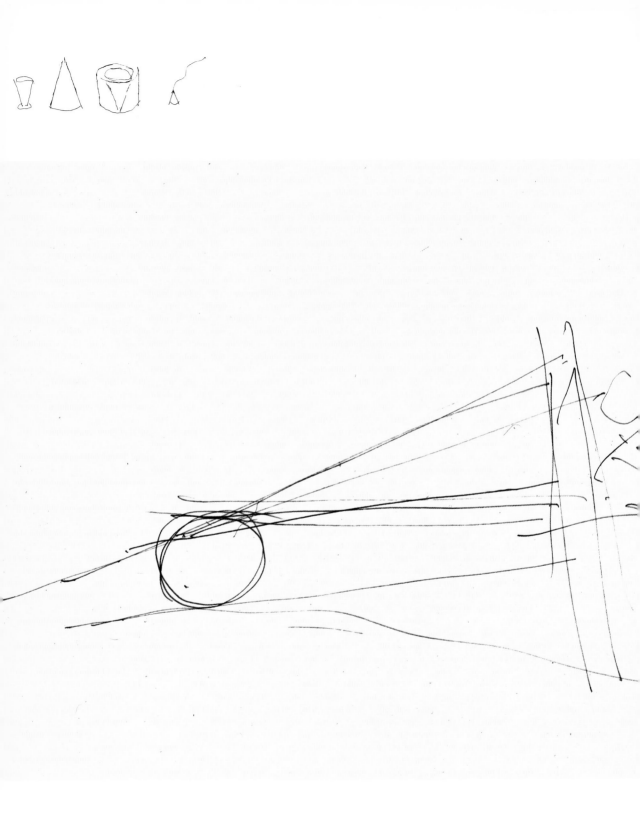

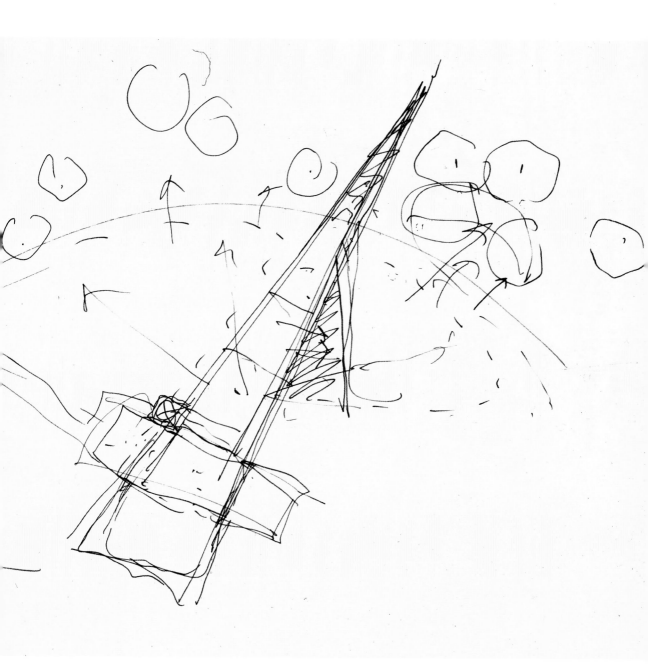

Landshark (lifeguard tower), Los Angeles, *1988* 85

86   Staglieno Cemetery, Genova, *1988*

Tree House   wood   Cave   House
              shelter
Hanging Tree   UFO/   conifer   Fire/
                    Ford   Demo
              M/Vally
Hot Spring Marsh

Hotel Santa Fe, Euro-Disney, Marne-la-Vallée, France, *1988* 87

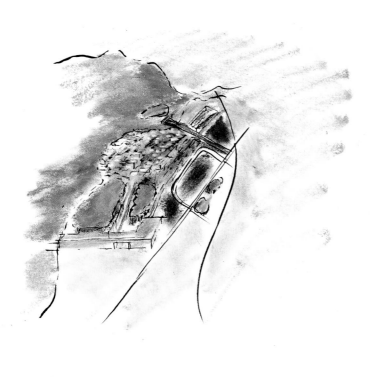

88 Mediterranean Hotel, Walt Disney World, Orlando, Florida, *1988*

90   University of California at Santa Cruz, *1989*

Rosenthal House, Manhattan Beach, California, *1990*

Kasbah

Rotation to mes
Sahat Magref Summer
Mag
Desert

Sunset
Dial

Shems

Mountain

Nachmed
Mountain

Oued

-South
Par

Necklace
of Water

City
Wall

point
to light

Rocks
dissolve

Bab Al-

(Orange

bat   Ksar

Cape

Jbel - Hajar

word
Agej
(Violence)

Exposure

Mountain
of
Sound

Sahara

Berber
Woman

Magreb

Trab.)

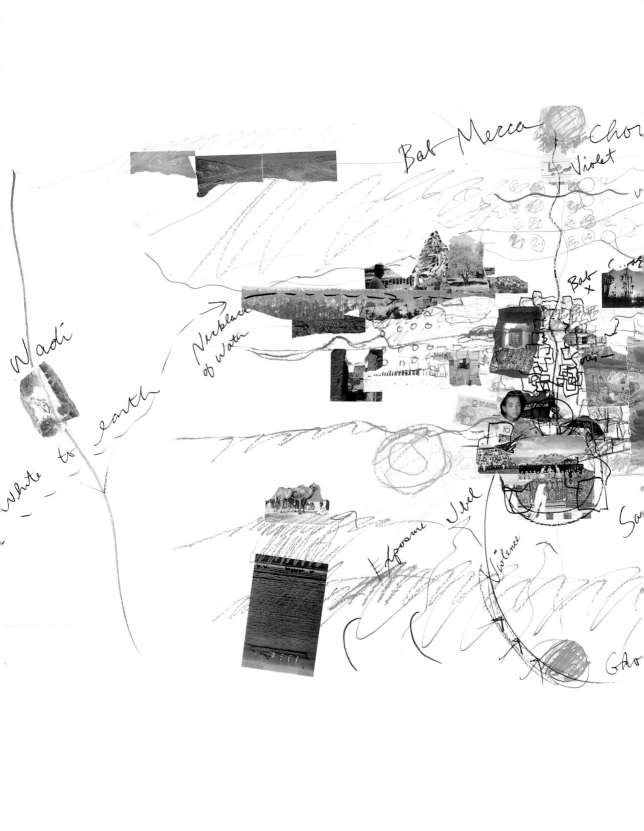

Bab Mecca   Chor
Violet

Wadi

white to earth

Necklace
of Water

Bab

Exposure Nel
Violence

Sa

Gao

Sydney Opera House, Sydney, Australia, *1990*   105

106 Atacama Desert, Chile, *1990*

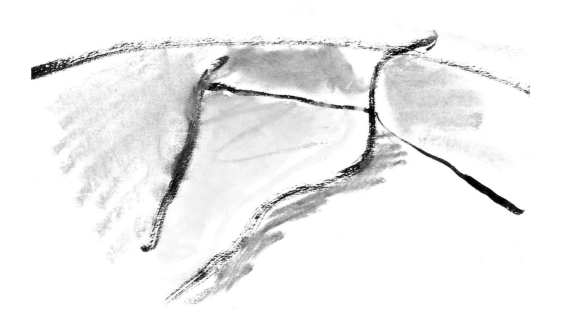

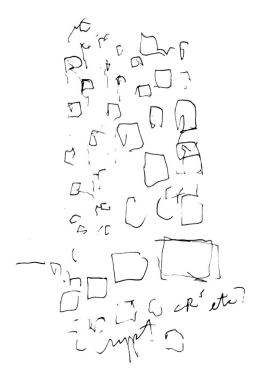

108   St. John the Divine, New York, *1991*

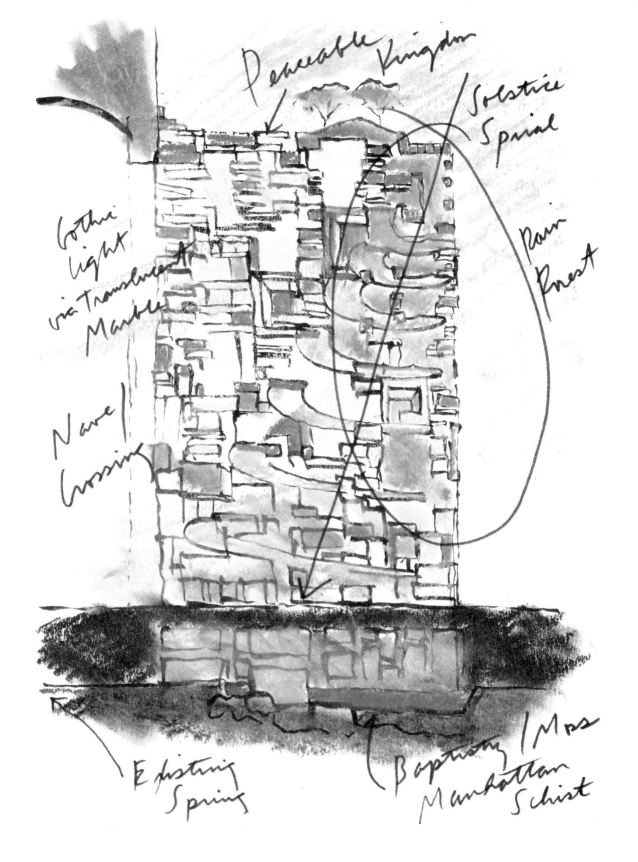

Peaceable Kingdom

Solstice Spiral

Gothic
Light
via Translucent
Marble

Rain
Forest

Nave
Crossing

Existing
Spring

Baptistry / Moss
Manhattan
Schist

Computerized sand
generate infinite variety
of blocks.
Spiral passes
Grape Arbor

112   Clark County Government Center, Las Vegas, Nevada, *1992*

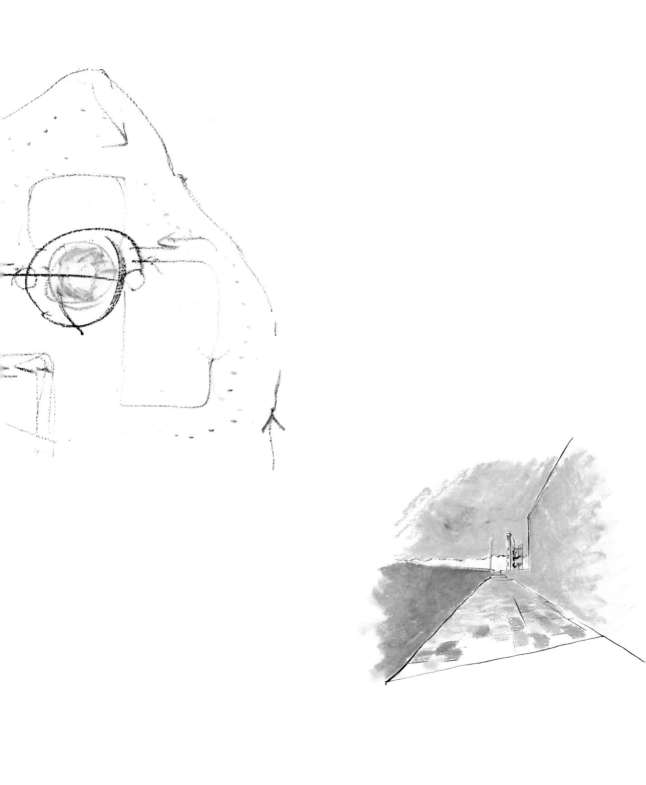

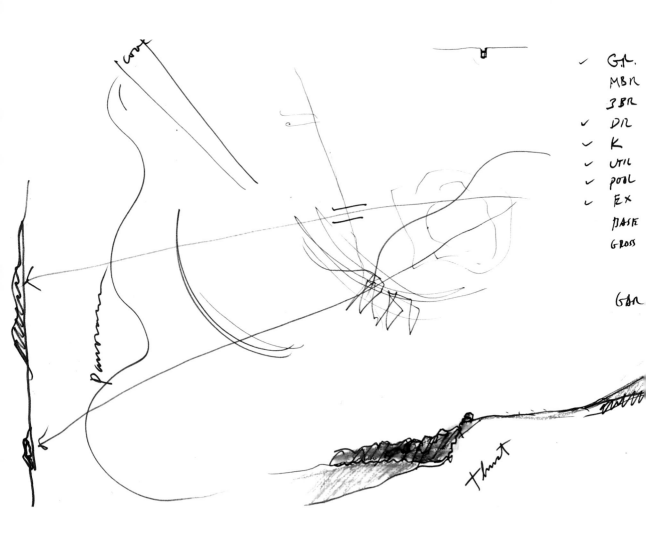

Gr.
MBR
3 BR
DR
K
UTIL
pool
EX
BASE
GROSS

GAR

court

Thrust

Picnic

Tree Dam / Chimney
light

Bridge G.R.

Cliff Dwelling

Tumble

116   Spencer Theater for the Performing Arts, Ruidoso, New Mexico, *1994*

118   Masada, Israel, *1994*

St. Catherine's Monastery, Sinai, *1994* 119

120   Dashur, Egypt, *1982, 1994*

List of works:

Pantheon, Rome
1985
4.75 x 6.25"
ink
p.01

Nelson Fine Arts
Center, Arizona State
University at Tempe
1985
9 x 12"
pastel and ink
p.02-03

Pisa, Italy
1991
5 x 6.25"
ink
p.05

Western Wall,
Jerusalem
1994
9.75 x 13"
pastel and ink
p.06

Meiji Shrine,
Tokyo
1990
9.75 x 13"
pastel and ink
p.06

Rio de Janeiro
1989
3.5 x 5"
pastel and ink
p.06

Airplane Window,
Georgia
1991
9.25 x 11"
pastel and ink
p.07

Paris
1965
11.75 x 9"
ink
p.07

Sant'Agnese, Rome
1985
5 x 6.25"
ink
p.08

Euro-Disney,
Marne-la-Valée,
France
1988
48 x 264"
collage, mixed
media
p.08-09

Notre Dame, Paris
1991
9.5 x 12.5"
pastel and ink
p.09

Agadir Palm Bay
Resort and Casino,
Agadir, Morocco
1990
9.5 x 12.5"
pastel
p.10

1990
36 x 60 x 2.25"
clay
p.10

University of
California at Davis
1990
3.5 x 5"
ink
p.11

1990
9.25 x 12.5"
pastel and ink
p.11

1990
8 x 15.5 x 2.375"
bronze
p.11

Rio Grande Valley,
New Mexico
1961
9 x 12"
ink
p.12-13

Madrigal de las
Altas Torres, Spain
1962
5 x 8"
watercolor
p.14

Monasterio de
Guisando, Spain
1962
7 x 6.75"
watercolor
p.15

Plaza Mayor,
Salamanca, Spain
1962
8.5 x 11.75"
ink
p.16-17

Acropolis, Athens
1962
8.5 x 11.75"
ink
p.18

1983
7 x 10.5"
ink
p.19

Leon Cathedral,
Spain
1962
8.5 x 11.75"
ink
p.20

Zaragoza, Spain
1962
8.5 x 11.75"
ink
p.21

Seville Cathedral,
Spain
1963
13 x 9"
ink
p.22

Malaga Cathedral,
Spain
1963
9.25 x 11.5"
ink
p.23

Costa Blanca, Spain
1963
8.5 x 11"
ink
p.24-25

Monte Albán, Mexico
1964
8.5 x 12"
ink
p.26-27

Teotihuacán, Mexico
1964
8.5 x 12"
ink
p.27

Chaco Canyon,
New Mexico
1964
9 x 12"
ink
p.28

La Luz Community,
Albuquerque,
New Mexico
1967
12 x 9"
ink
p.29

Chartres, France
1981
4.75 x 6.75"
ink
p.30

1981
5 x 11.5"
ink
p.30

1982
4.75 x 6.75"
ink
p.30

1981
4 x 6"
watercolor
p.31

Chenonceaux, France
1982
4.75 x 6.75"
ink
p.32-33

Rocamadour, France
1982
9 x 11.5"
ink
p.34-35

Segovia, Spain
1982
9 x 11.5"
ink
p.36-37

Desert Highlands,
Phoenix, Arizona
1983
9 x 12.5"
marker and ink
p.38

1983
70 x 47"
pen and ink on
trace
p.39

Les Baux de
Provence, France
1982
9 x 11.5"
ink
p.40

Venice
1985
5 x 6.25"
pastel and ink
p.41

Il Tempietto, Rome
1985
3.5 x 4.5"
ink
p.42

Trinità dei Monti,
Rome
1985
5 x 6.25"
ink
p.43

Rome
1985
9.25 x 12.25"
pastel and ink
p.44-45

Porta Maggiore,
Rome
1985
9.25 x 12.25"
ink
p.46-47

1985
12.5 x 9.5"
pastel and ink
p.48

Tomb of Eurysaces,
Rome
1985
12.25 x 9.25"
pastel and ink
p.49

Tuscolo, Italy
1985
9.5 x 12.5"
pastel and ink
p.50

Basilica of
Maxentius, Rome
1985
12.5 x 9.25"
pastel and ink
p.51

Mount Etna, Italy
1985
9.5 x 12.5"
pastel and ink
p.52

Umbria, Italy
1985
4.75 x 6.25"
ink
p.53

Grotto of Tiberius,
Italy
1985
9.5 x 12.5"
pastel and ink
p.54

San Leo, Italy
1985
12.5 x 9.5"
pastel and ink
p.55

Duomo, Orvieto, Italy
1985
12.5 x 9.5"
pastel and ink
p.56

Trajan's Market,
Rome
1985
5 x 6.25"
pastel and ink
p.57

Temple of Apollo,
Rome
1985
9.25 x 12.25"
pastel and ink
p.58-59

Temple of Castor and
Pollux, Rome
1985
6.25 x 5"
ink
p.59

Hadrian's Villa,
Tivoli, Italy
1985
12.5 x 9.5"
pastel and ink
p.60

Temple of Apollo,
Rome
1985
12.5 x 9.5"
pastel and ink
p.61

Pyramid of Caio
Cestio, Rome
1985
4.75 x 6.25"
pastel and ink
p.62-63

Nelson Fine Arts
Center, Arizona State
University at Tempe
1985
9.5 x 12.5"
ink
p.64

1985
9.5 x 12.5"
pastel and ink
p.65

Las Vegas Library
and Children's
Museum, Las Vegas,
Nevada
1986
3.4 x 4.5"
ink
p.66

1986
9 x 11.75"
ink
p.66

1986
12 x 9"
pastel and ink
p.67

American Heritage
Center and Art
Museum, University
of Wyoming
at Laramie
1986
9 x 11.75"
ink
p.68

1986
20 x 30"
marker
p.69

1986
9 x 12"
pastel and ink
p.70

1986
5 x 5"
ink
p.71

1986
9 x 12.5"
pastel and ink
p.71

Charleston Aquarium,
Charleston,
South Carolina
1986
24 x 30"
marker
p.72

1986
21 x 23.75"
pastel and ink
p.73

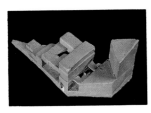

Classroom,
Laboratory,
Administration
Building, California
Polytechnic State
University at Ponoma
1987
30 x 96"
ink
p.74-75

1987
9 x 12"
pastel and ink
p.76-77

Turtle Creek House,
Dallas
1987
12 x 9"
pastel and ink
p.78

1987
11 x 8.5"
ink
p.79

Incense Burner
1987
4 x 6"
ink
p.80

Mesa Public Library,
Los Alamos,
New Mexico
1987
12 x 34.75"
ink on trace
p.80-81

1987
9.5 x 12.5"
pastel and ink
p.82-83

Ship of the Desert,
Nevada
1988
9 x 12"
pastel and ink
p.83

Landshark (lifeguard
tower), Los Angeles
1988
9.5 x 12.5"
pastel and ink
p.84

1988
12 x 9"
pastel and ink
p.85

Staglieno Cemetery,
Genova
1988
12 x 8.75"
pastel and ink
p.86

Hotel Santa Fe,
Euro-Disney,
Marne-la-Valée,
France
1988
8.75 x 8.5"
ink
p.87

1988
9 x 12"
pastel and ink
p.87

Mediterranean Hotel,
Walt Disney World,
Orlando, Florida
1988
9 x 12"
pastel and ink
p.88

1988
9 x 11.5"
pastel and ink
p.88-89

University of
California at
Santa Cruz
1989
9 x 12"
pastel and ink
p.90-91

Rosenthal House,
Manhattan Beach,
California
1990
9.75 x 13"
pastel and ink
p.92

1990
9.75 x 13"
pastel and ink
p.93

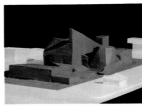

Arizona Museum of Science,
Phoenix
1990
52.75 x 82.5"
collage, mixed
media
p.94-95

Agadir Palm Bay
Resort and Casino,
Agadir, Morocco
1990
9 x 12"
pastel and ink
p.96-97

1990
52.75 x 172.5"
collage, mixed
media
p.98-99

1990
9.5 x 12.5"
pastel and ink
p.100

1990
9.5 x 12.5"
pastel and ink
p.101

Tampa Museum of
Science and Industry,
Tampa, Florida
1990
9 x 21.75"
pastel and ink
p.102-103

St. Louis, Missouri
1990
3.5 x 4.75"
ink
p.104

Sydney Opera House,
Sydney, Australia
1990
3.5 x 4.75"
ink
p.105

Atacama Desert,
Chile
1990
9 x 12"
pastel and ink
p.106

Aragon, Spain
1991
9 x 10.5"
pastel and ink
p.107

St. John the Divine,
New York
1991
8 x 5"
ink
p.108

1991
8 x 5"
ink
p.108

1991
12 x 9"
pastel and ink
p.109

1991
12.5 x 9.5"
pastel and ink
p.110

1991
12 x 9"
pastel and ink
p.111

Clark County
Government Center,
Las Vegas, Nevada
1992
24 x 53
crayon and pastel
p.112-113

1992
11 x 14"
pastel and ink
p.113

House, Beverly,
Massachusetts
1992
36 x 115"
pastel and marker
p.114-115

Spencer Theater for
the Performing Arts,
Ruidoso, New Mexico
1994
9.5 x 12.5"
pastel and ink
p.116

Tikal, Guatemala
1994
13 x 9.75"
pastel and ink
p.117

Masada, Israel
1994
9.75 x 13"
pastel and ink
p.118-119

St. Catherine's
Monastery, Sinai
1994
9.75 x 13"
pastel and ink
p.119

Dashur, Egypt
1982
7 x 9.5"
ink
p.120

1994
9.75 x 13"
pastel and ink
p.120-121

Karnak, Egypt
1994
9.75 x 13"
pastel and ink
p.122-123

1994
9.75 x 13"
pastel and ink
p.123

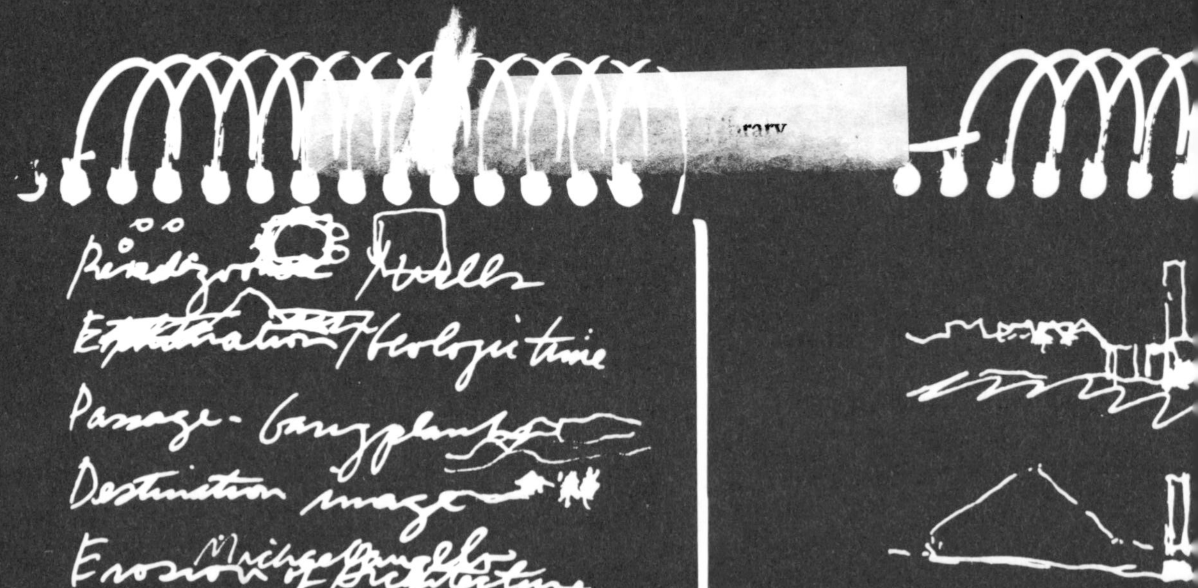
Geologic time
Passage -
Destination image
Image in Snow
Product
Wild West assertion of
Monumentality